WORDS THAT SHAPED AMERICA

THE MOST POWERFUL WORDS ABOUT WOMEN'S RIGHTS

VOTES FOR WOMEN

BY JANEY LEVY

Gareth Stevens PUBLISHING

Please visit our website, www.garethstevens.com. For a free color catalog of all our high-quality books, call toll free 1-800-542-2595 or fax 1-877-542-2596.

Library of Congress Cataloging-in-Publication Data

Names: Levy, Janey, author.
Title: The most powerful words about women's rights / Janey Levy.
Description: New York : Gareth Stevens Publishing, 2020. | Series: Words that shaped America | Includes index.
Identifiers: LCCN 2019027324 | ISBN 9781538248089 (6 Pack) | ISBN 9781538248096 (library binding) | ISBN 9781538248072 (paperback) | ISBN 9781538248102 (ebook)
Subjects: LCSH: Women's rights--History--Juvenile literature.
Classification: LCC HQ1236 .L489 2020 | DDC 305.4209--dc23
LC record available at https://lccn.loc.gov/2019027324

First Edition

Published in 2020 by
Gareth Stevens Publishing
111 East 14th Street, Suite 349
New York, NY 10003

Designer: Sarah Liddell
Editor: Therese Shea

Photo credits: Cover, pp. 1 (main), 17 (march) Fœ/Wikimedia Commons; cover, pp. 1 (inset), 11 (Declaration of Sentiments) photo courtesy of Library of Congress; ink smear used throughout Itsmesimon/Shutterstock.com; border used throughout igorrita/Shutterstock.com; background used throughout Lukasz Szwaj/Shutterstock.com; p. 5 MSClaudiu/Wikimedia Commons; p. 7 (Judith Sargent Murray) Oxxo/Wikimedia Commons; p. 7 (Abigail Adams) Pateca/Wikimedia Commons; p. 9 David Levy/Wikimedia Commons; p. 11 (Lucretia Mott) Jan Arkesteijn/Wikimedia Commons; p. 13 KellyDoyle/Wikimedia Commons; p. 14 Universal History Archive/Contirbutor/Universal Images Group/Getty Images; p. 15 Scewing/Wikimedia Commons; p. 17 (flyer) Adam Cuerden/Wikimedia Commons; p. 19 LynnGilbert5/Wikimedia Commons; p. 21 John Olson/Contributor/The LIFE Picture Collection/Getty Images; p. 22 AFP/Stringer/AFP/Getty Images; p. 23 Denver Post/Contributor/Denver Post/Getty Images; p. 25 (photo) Monica Schipper/Stringer/Getty Images Entertainment/Getty Images; p. 25 (magazine) Missvain/Wikimedia Commons; p. 27 Bettmann/Contributor/Gettmann/Getty Images.

Printed in the United States of America

CONTENTS

Words in the glossary appear in **bold** type the first time they are used in the text.

WHAT DOES "WOMEN'S RIGHTS" MEAN?

How would *you* begin to discuss women's rights? You could start by establishing the term's meaning. The saying "women's rights are human rights" was first declared at a United Nations (UN) conference in 1993. So, what are human rights?

The UN identifies human rights as rights belonging to everyone, regardless of race, sex, nationality, language, or religion. In 1948, the UN listed those rights in the Universal Declaration of Human Rights. Among them are the right to life and liberty, freedom of expression, the rights to work and to education, the right to equal pay for equal work, and the right to take part in government.

BEHIND THE WORDS

THE FIRST KNOWN USE OF THE TERM "WOMEN'S RIGHTS" WAS IN 1632.

Yet, women have long lacked full human rights. This book explores the powerful words that have inspired and advanced the struggle for women's rights.

A TREATY FOR WOMEN'S RIGHTS

In 1979, the UN adopted the Convention on the Elimination of All Forms of **Discrimination** Against Women. It became an international treaty after 20 countries approved it in 1981. One passage from it states that countries "shall take in all fields . . . all appropriate measures . . . to ensure the full development and advancement of women, for the purpose of guaranteeing them the exercise and enjoyment of human rights and fundamental freedoms on the basis of equality with men."

THE UNIVERSAL DECLARATION OF Human Rights

WHEREAS recognition of the inherent dignity and of the equal and inalienable rights of all members of the human family is the foundation of freedom, justice and peace in the world,

WHEREAS disregard and contempt for human rights have resulted in barbarous acts which have outraged the conscience of mankind, and the advent of a world in which human beings shall enjoy freedom of speech and belief and freedom from fear and want has been proclaimed as the highest aspiration of the common people,

WHEREAS it is essential, if man is not to be compelled to have recourse, as a last resort, to rebellion against tyranny and oppression, that human rights should be protected by the rule of law,

WHEREAS it is essential to promote the development of friendly relations among nations,

WHEREAS the peoples of the United Nations have in the Charter reaffirmed their faith in fundamental human rights, in the dignity and worth of the human person and in the equal rights of men and women and have determined to promote social progress and better standards of life in larger freedom,

WHEREAS Member States have pledged themselves to achieve, in co-operation with the United Nations, the promotion of universal respect for and observance of human rights and fundamental freedoms,

WHEREAS a common understanding of these rights and freedoms is of the greatest importance for the full realization of this pledge,

NOW THEREFORE THE GENERAL ASSEMBLY PROCLAIMS this Universal Declaration of Human Rights as a common standard of achievement for all peoples and all nations, to the end that every individual and every organ of society, keeping this Declaration constantly in mind, shall strive by teaching and education to promote respect for these rights and freedoms and by progressive measures, national and international, to secure their universal and effective recognition and observance, both among the peoples of Member States themselves and among the peoples of territories under their jurisdiction.

UNITED NATIONS

The Universal Declaration of Human Rights was written by representatives from all over the world and has been translated into over 500 languages.

"REMEMBER THE LADIES"

Abigail Adams (1744–1818) was the wife of John Adams, the second US president. When John was away in 1776 helping write the Declaration of Independence, she wrote him, requesting that he **advocate** for women's rights: "[I]n the new Code of Laws which I suppose it will be necessary for you to make I desire you would Remember the Ladies, and be more generous and favourable to them than your ancestors."

Abigail also warned, "If perticular care and attention is not paid to the Ladies we are determined to foment [rouse] a Rebelion, and will not hold ourselves bound by any laws in which we have no voice, or Representation." Despite her words, the laws for the new nation didn't include women's rights.

BEHIND THE WORDS

ABIGAIL WANTED THE LAWS OF THE NEW UNITED STATES TO PROVIDE GREATER PROTECTION FOR WOMEN. SHE ALSO WANTED WOMEN TO BE ABLE TO RECEIVE A FORMAL EDUCATION.

OTHER EARLY VOICES

Abigail Adams wasn't alone in promoting women's rights during this period. In 1764, American patriot James Otis wrote, "Are not women born as free as men? Would it not be infamous [shameful] to **assert** that the ladies are all slaves by nature?" In 1775, patriot Thomas Paine supported women's rights in an article for *Pennsylvania Magazine*. And in 1791, women's rights advocate Judith Sargent Murray wrote an essay titled "On the Equality of the Sexes."

JUDITH SARGENT MURRAY

ABIGAIL ADAMS

LIKE OTHER WOMEN OF HER TIME, ABIGAIL LACKED A FORMAL EDUCATION. BUT SHE MADE USE OF HER FAMILY'S LIBRARY TO EDUCATE HERSELF.

THE DECLARATION OF SENTIMENTS

Sixty-five years after the British colonies won their independence in the American Revolution, women still couldn't vote and lacked many other rights. On July 13, 1848, Elizabeth Cady Stanton was discussing her unhappiness about the situation with four female friends over tea.

Within 2 days, the women had decided to hold a convention, or meeting, on the topic of women's rights, chosen a date, found a location, and placed a newspaper announcement. The notice announced "A convention to discuss the social, civil, and religious condition and rights of woman." It was scheduled to take place in Seneca Falls, New York, on July 19 and 20, 1848. Stanton prepared a statement of women's complaints titled the Declaration of Sentiments.

BEHIND THE WORDS

BEFORE THE 1848 CONVENTION, NO PUBLIC MEETING ON WOMEN'S RIGHTS HAD EVER BEEN CALLED BEFORE IN THE HISTORY OF WESTERN CIVILIZATION!

ELIZABETH CADY STANTON (1815-1902)

Stanton was born November 12, 1815, in Johnstown, New York. Her parents were well-known citizens, and she received an excellent education. She learned about law from her father, a lawyer. In 1840, she married abolitionist Henry Stanton and became active in the fight against slavery. Abolitionist Lucretia Mott helped Elizabeth organize the Seneca Falls convention. Over time, Stanton became especially concerned with women's **suffrage**, and she worked closely with Susan B. Anthony on this cause.

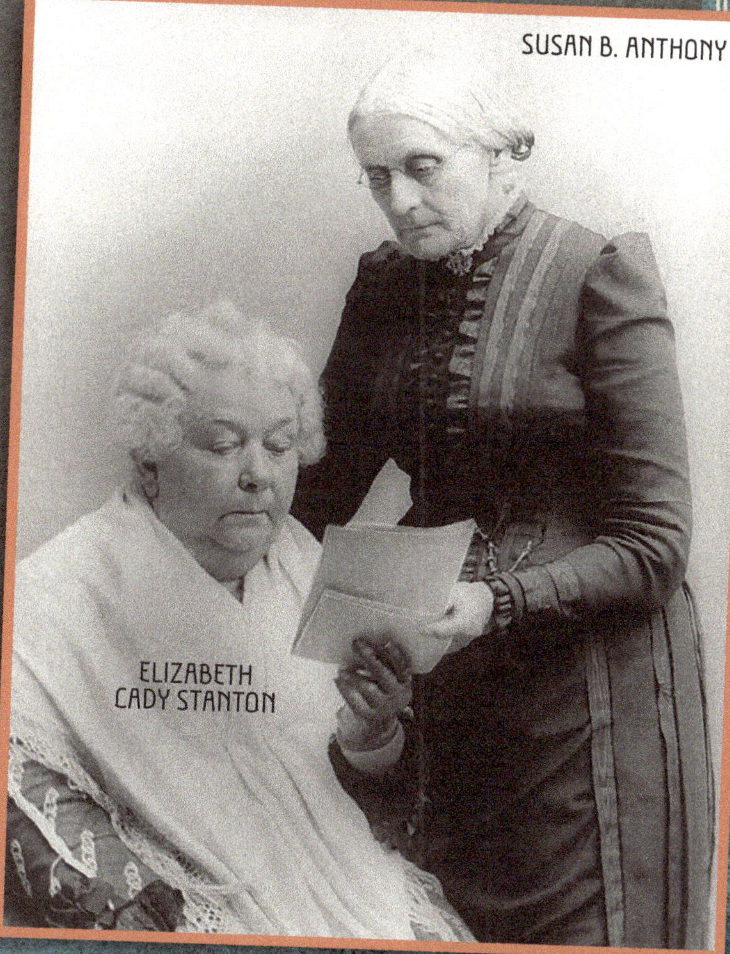

Stanton died 18 years before American women won the right to vote.

Here are some of the complaints Stanton listed in the Declaration:

> "The history of mankind is a history of repeated injuries and **usurpations** on the part of man toward woman, having in direct object the establishment of an absolute tyranny over her. . .
>
> He has never permitted her to exercise her **inalienable** right to the elective franchise [right to vote].
>
> He has compelled her to submit to laws, in the formation of which she had no voice.
>
> He has withheld from her rights which are given to the most ignorant and degraded [dishonorable] men."

Newspapers attacked the women, but the movement started by Stanton, Mott, and others grew. People across the nation discussed the issues the women raised, and more women's rights conventions were held.

BEHIND THE WORDS

STANTON MODELED THE DECLARATION OF SENTIMENTS ON THE DECLARATION OF INDEPENDENCE, A DOCUMENT THAT WAS THE SYMBOL OF AMERICAN FREEDOM.

LUCRETIA MOTT

THE DECLARATION OF SENTIMENTS WAS VOTED ON AND APPROVED BY THOSE WHO ATTENDED THE SENECA FALLS CONVENTION.

Our Roll of Honor
Containing all the
Signatures to the "Declaration of Sentiments"
Set Forth by the First
Woman's Rights Convention,
held at
Seneca Falls, New York
July 19-20, 1848

LADIES:

Lucretia Mott
Harriet Cady Eaton
Margaret Pryor
Elizabeth Cady Stanton
Eunice Newton Foote
Mary Ann M'Clintock
Margaret Schooley
Martha C. Wright
Jane C. Hunt
Amy Post
Catherine F. Stebbins
Mary Ann Frink
Lydia Mount
Delia Mathews
Catherine C. Paine
Elizabeth W. M'Clintock
Malvina Seymour
Phebe Mosher
Catherine Shaw
Deborah Scott
Sarah Hallowell
Mary M'Clintock
Mary Gilbert
Sophronia Taylor
Cynthia Davis
Hannah Plant
Lucy Jones
Sarah Whitney
Mary H. Hallowell
Elizabeth Conklin
Sally Pitcher
Mary Conklin
Susan Quinn
Mary S. Mirror
Phebe King
Julia Ann Drake
Charlotte Woodward
Martha Underhill
Dorothy Mathews
Eunice Barker
Sarah R. Woods
Lydia Gild
Sarah Hoffman
Elizabeth Leslie
Martha Ridley
Rachel D. Bonnel
Betsey Tewksbury
Rhoda Palmer
Margaret Jenkins
Cynthia Fuller
Mary Martin
P. A. Culvert
Susan R. Doty
Rebecca Race
Sarah A. Mosher
Mary E. Vail
Lucy Spalding
Lovina Latham
Sarah Smith
Eliza Martin
Maria E. Wilbur
Elizabeth D. Smith
Caroline Barker
Ann Porter
Experience Gibbs
Antoinette E. Segur
Hannah J. Latham
Sarah Sisson

GENTLEMEN:

Richard P. Hunt
Samuel D. Tillman
Justin Williams
Elisha Foote
Frederick Douglass
Henry W. Seymour
Henry Seymour
David Spalding
William G. Barker
Elias J. Doty
John Jones
William S. Dell
James Mott
William Burroughs
Robert Smallbridge
Jacob Mathews
Charles L. Hoskins
Thomas M'Clintock
Saron Phillips
Jacob P. Chamberlain
Jonathan Metcalf
Nathan J. Milliken
S. E. Woodworth
Edward F. Underhill
George W. Pryor
Joel Bunker
Isaac VanTassel
Thomas Dell
E. W. Capron
Stephen Shear
Henry Hatley
Azaliah Schooley

SHOULD WOMEN VOTE?

It may seem hard to believe today, but the idea that women should vote was the subject of much controversy, or disagreement, in 1848. Even Stanton's good friend Lucretia Mott was shocked by the suggestion. Stanton herself wasn't able to persuade people at the convention to support the proposal. Only the great abolitionist speaker Frederick Douglass convinced enough people. He declared, "Suffrage is the power to choose rulers and make laws, and the right by which all others are secured."

"AIN'T I A WOMAN?"

In 1851, another women's rights convention, inspired by the Seneca Falls convention, was held in Akron, Ohio. It was at this convention that one of the most famous women's rights speeches in American history was delivered. The woman who delivered it was Sojourner Truth.

BEHIND THE WORDS

TRUTH'S RELIGIOUS FAITH GAVE HER THE STRENGTH SHE NEEDED TO WALK AWAY FROM HER CRUEL MASTER.

Sojourner Truth was born into slavery but escaped. As she later said, "I did not run away. I walked away by daylight." She became a wandering preacher and was also an abolitionist and advocate for women's rights. Although Truth never learned to read or write, she was a powerful speaker. She was on a speaking tour in 1851 when she appeared at the Ohio convention and gave the speech that became famous. It's known as the "Ain't I a Woman?" speech.

SOJOURNER TRUTH (1797-1883)

Sojourner Truth was born in Ulster County, New York, as Isabella Baumfree. She was bought and sold four times, performed hard physical labor, and suffered harsh punishments. She was forced into marriage around 1815 and had five children. She left her owner in 1827 and went to a nearby abolitionist family, who bought her freedom. In 1828, she moved to New York City and worked for a minister. She began preaching in 1843 and changed her name to Sojourner Truth.

SOJOURNER TRUTH MET ELIZABETH CADY STANTON AS WELL AS SUSAN B. ANTHONY.

Sojourner Truth's 1851 speech was short but powerful. Here's part of what she had to say: "That man over there says that women need to be helped into carriages and lifted over ditches, and to have the best place everywhere. Nobody ever helps me into carriages, over mud-puddles, gives me any best place! And ain't I a woman? Look at me! Look at my arm! I have ploughed [plowed] and planted, and gathered into barns, and no man could head [beat] me! And ain't I a woman?"

Truth's speech didn't bring about immediate change, but she continued to advocate for the rights of women and African Americans. She helped slaves escape to freedom, and, after the **American Civil War** started, she urged young men to fight for the North.

WOMEN'S STRENGTH

In her "Ain't I a Woman" speech, Truth challenged the idea that women weren't equal to men because they were inferior. She pointed out that men said women needed help because they were weak and delicate, but no one had ever treated her that way. And, in fact, she was able to work as well as any man. Clearly women weren't the inferior, weak, delicate creatures men claimed they were, she argued.

This is how Sojourner Truth looked at the time of the Civil War.

BEHIND THE WORDS

In spite of the famous speech's name, a version, or form, of the speech published a month after it was given doesn't include the phrase "Ain't I a woman."

THE NINETEENTH AMENDMENT

Thanks to Sojourner Truth, Elizabeth Cady Stanton, and countless others, support grew for an amendment to the US Constitution to allow women to vote. In 1918, the amendment passed in the House of Representatives but didn't pass in the Senate. However, in 1919, it was finally approved in both parts of Congress and, in 1920, was approved by enough states to become law. The Nineteenth Amendment stated: "The right of citizens of the United States to vote shall not be denied or abridged by the United States or by any State on account of sex."

However, the amendment didn't guarantee other rights women had lacked before or improve women's position in other ways in society. There were still obstacles to overcome.

BEHIND THE WORDS

THE NINETEENTH AMENDMENT GUARANTEES THAT NO US GOVERNMENT CAN ABRIDGE, OR RESTRICT, A WOMAN'S RIGHT TO VOTE IN ANY WAY.

THE FIRST SUFFRAGE MARCH IN WASHINGTON, DC, TOOK PLACE ON MARCH 3, 1913. MORE THAN 5,000 WOMEN MARCHED FOR THE RIGHT TO VOTE.

STATE BY STATE

The Nineteenth Amendment needed to be ratified, or approved, by 36 states in order to become law. Several states were against it, so many believed it would fail. However, on August 18, 1920, Tennessee became the thirty-sixth state to pass it. On August 26, 1920, the Nineteenth Amendment officially became part of the US Constitution. American women could finally vote. It took some states many years to ratify the amendment. Mississippi was the last in 1984.

THE FEMININE MYSTIQUE

An important book of the 20th-century women's rights, or feminist, movement appeared in 1963. It was Betty Friedan's *The Feminine Mystique*. Friedan invented the term "feminine mystique" to describe the idea that women should be happy living a life devoted to housework, raising children, and caring for a husband.

Friedan called the unhappiness that resulted from being unable to live up to the feminine mystique the "problem that has no name." She described it as "a strange stirring, a sense of dissatisfaction, a yearning that women suffered in the middle of the twentieth century in the United States. . . . They were taught to pity the **neurotic**, unfeminine, unhappy women who wanted to be poets or physicists or presidents. They learned that truly feminine women do not want careers, higher education, political rights."

Betty Friedan (1921–2006)

Friedan was born Bettye Goldstein on February 4, 1921, in Peoria, Illinois. She graduated from Smith College in 1942 and then studied at the University of California Berkeley. She married Carl Friedan in 1947, and they had three children. In 1966, she became one of the founders of the National Organization for Women (NOW). She helped found the National Women's Political **Caucus** in 1971. Some consider her the "mother" of the modern women's rights movement.

BETTY FRIEDAN

MANY WOMEN RECOGNIZED THEIR UNHAPPINESS IN BETTY FRIEDAN'S *THE FEMININE MYSTIQUE*. IT BECAME A BEST SELLER, INSPIRING THE MODERN WOMEN'S RIGHTS MOVEMENT.

BEHIND THE WORDS

"MYSTIQUE" IS A WORD WHICH MEANS A QUALITY OF MYSTERY OR A MYSTERIOUS POWER SURROUNDING A CERTAIN OCCUPATION OR PURSUIT.

OUR BODIES, OURSELVES

It may be hard to believe in the internet age, but information about women's health hasn't always been readily available to women, and doctors haven't always been helpful. This included very basic facts about a woman's body and how it works. So in 1969, 12 women decided to do something about that. They formed what came to be called the Boston Women's Health Collective.

In 1970, the women published their first effort to fill the gap in women's health information: a booklet called *Women and Their Bodies*. The women designed the booklet as a "course on health, women and our bodies." The booklet wasn't fancy. The pages were just stapled together. The title page and table of contents were handwritten. But changes in the next 2 years helped spread its popularity.

BEHIND THE WORDS

WOMEN AND THEIR BODIES WAS PRESENTED AS A COURSE FOR WOMEN IN BOSTON, MASSACHUSETTS. IT WAS CREATED SO IT COULD BE SHARED WITH WOMEN'S HEALTH GROUPS BEYOND BOSTON.

THE BEGINNINGS

The women of the collective described how the booklet came about: "The **impetus** for this course grew out of a workshop . . . at a women's conference at Emmanuel College in Boston, May 1969. After that, several of us developed a questionnaire about women's feelings about their bodies and their relationship to doctors. We discovered . . . we had to learn for ourselves. We talked about our own experiences and we shared our own knowledge."

THE WOMEN BEHIND *WOMEN AND THEIR BODIES* KNEW THAT HEALTH CARE AND WOMEN'S RIGHTS WERE CONNECTED. THE PROJECT WAS ANOTHER EXAMPLE OF WOMEN UNITING TO HELP EACH OTHER.

In 1971, the booklet became a book. It was published by the New England Free Press and sold 250,000 copies. Those copies weren't sold through a traditional advertising campaign, the way books usually are. They were sold because people told others about the book.

Another big change happened in 1971 as well. The title of the book became *Our Bodies, Ourselves*. The women of the collective chose those words—"our bodies, ourselves"—for a reason. They wanted women to know they had a right to make choices about their health care. In order to do that, women need to take full responsibility for their body. They need to know their body, how it works, and what it needs to stay healthy.

THE FIRST COMMERCIAL **EDITION** OF *OUR BODIES, OURSELVES* APPEARED IN 1973. ONE OF THE AUTHORS, DIANE SIEGAL, IS SHOWN HERE WITH A LATER BOOK *OURSELVES, GROWING OLDER*.

BEHIND THE WORDS

OUR BODIES, OURSELVES WAS SUCH AN INFLUENTIAL BOOK THAT THE LIBRARY OF CONGRESS INCLUDED IT IN A 2012 EXHIBIT TITLED *BOOKS THAT SHAPED AMERICA*. ALSO FEATURED WAS *THE FEMININE MYSTIQUE*.

WORLDWIDE INFLUENCE

Our Bodies, Ourselves wasn't just a highly influential book in the United States. It had an enormous influence around the world. By 2018, it had been translated into 31 languages and reached millions of women. It was first translated into Spanish, but over the years, it has also been translated into languages such as Japanese, Danish, Greek, Russian, Chinese, Armenian, Bulgarian, Serbian, Romanian, Albanian, and Nepali.

THE NATIONAL WOMEN'S POLITICAL CAUCUS

The year 1971 was a big one for women's rights. Not only did *Our Bodies, Ourselves* appear for the first time under that title, but the National Women's Political Caucus held its organizing conference in July of that year. Over 320 women from 26 states attended the meeting.

The caucus's goal was—and is—to increase women's participation in government, such as electing women to government office and having them appointed as judges. The statement of purpose from the organizing conference calls for the caucus to take action "against sexism, racism, institutional violence and poverty."

BEHIND THE WORDS

THE FOUNDERS OF THE CAUCUS BELIEVED THE BEST WAY TO ADDRESS ISSUES THAT CONCERN WOMEN—SUCH AS **SEXISM**, RACISM, VIOLENCE, AND POVERTY—WAS MORE WOMEN LAWMAKERS.

Besides Betty Friedan, another founder of the caucus was the influential feminist writer and speaker Gloria Steinem. Steinem gave a speech to the caucus that became famous.

GLORIA STEINEM

Steinem was born on March 25, 1934, in Toledo, Ohio. Because her father was a wandering salesman and the family was always traveling, Steinem didn't spend a full year in school until she was 12 years old. She graduated from Smith College in 1956. After 2 years in India, she returned to the United States and became a writer. She helped found *New York magazine* as well as *Ms.* magazine.

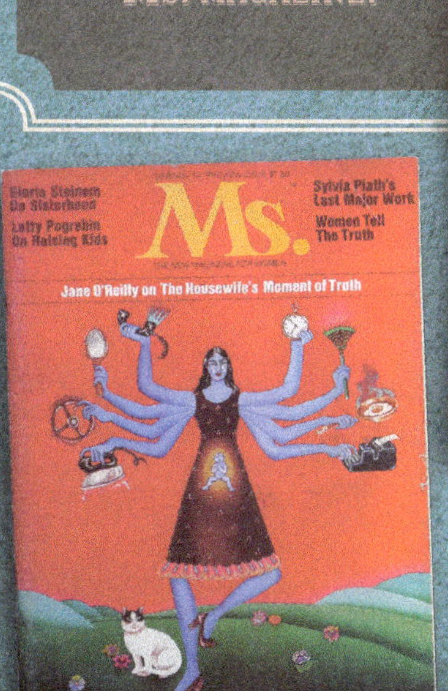

IN 1971, STEINEM FOUNDED A MAGAZINE FOR WOMEN—CALLED MS.—WITH AFRICAN AMERICAN **ACTIVIST** DOROTHY PITMAN HUGHES.

"ADDRESS TO THE WOMEN OF AMERICA"

Gloria Steinem delivered her speech to the National Women's Political Caucus conference on July 10, 1971. She spoke about the revolutionary nature of what the women's movement was proposing: a society in which no one would be treated as worth less just because they were female or had dark skin.

She said, "This is no simple reform. It really is a revolution. Sex and race, because they are easy, visible differences, have been the primary ways of organizing human beings into superior and inferior groups, and into the cheap labor on which this system still depends. We are talking about a society in which there will be no roles other than those chosen, or those earned. We are really talking about **humanism**."

This revolution hasn't achieved its goals, but feminists remain hopeful.

BEHIND THE WORDS

IN 1971, THERE WERE ONLY 15 WOMEN IN CONGRESS. THAT'S OUT OF 435 MEMBERS IN THE HOUSE OF REPRESENTATIVES AND 100 SENATORS IN THE SENATE.

SPEAKERS AT THE NATIONAL WOMEN'S POLITICAL CAUCUS

SLOWLY, THE WORK OF THE NATIONAL WOMEN'S POLITICAL CAUCUS IS PAYING OFF. THE 116TH CONGRESS, WHICH BEGAN IN JANUARY 2019, HAD A RECORD NUMBER OF WOMEN: 102 IN THE HOUSE OF REPRESENTATIVES AND 25 IN THE SENATE. THREE WOMEN SIT ON THE US SUPREME COURT.

MORE ABOUT THE NATIONAL WOMEN'S POLITICAL CAUCUS

The caucus's statement of purpose has other important things to say as well. It includes a promise to gather and train feminist female candidates for government office. It undertakes to reform the rules and structures of the political parties so that women have equal decision-making power. It also promises to register more women voters, raise women's issues in all elections, and work for legislation that meets women's needs.

#METOO AND TIME'S UP

The struggle for women's rights continues today. Two contemporary movements are part of this continuing struggle.

#MeToo fights to protect women from being touched in unwanted ways and from unwelcome comments about their bodies. The hashtag took off when actress Alyssa Milano told her followers on Twitter to "write 'me too' as a reply to this tweet" if they'd experienced unwelcome contact or comments.

Time's Up is focused on the workplace. It advises that issues in the workplace can be solved only through equality. The group fights for equal pay and more opportunities for women and people of color.

BEHIND THE WORDS

OVER 66,000 USERS RESPONDED TO ALYSSA MILANO'S TWEET.

Everyone today can be part of the fight for women's rights. Because when rights are equal for everyone, everyone wins.

MORE ON WOMEN'S RIGHTS TODAY

A group called Women's March is also fighting for women's rights today. They "believe that Women's Rights are Human Rights and Human Rights are Women's Rights." Much of what this group believes in is familiar because they're continuing battles begun earlier by other groups. The group is fighting for women's health care, to end violence against women, and for equal pay for women, among other things.

A TIMELINE OF THE STRUGGLE FOR WOMEN'S RIGHTS

1776: ABIGAIL ADAMS TELLS JOHN ADAMS TO "REMEMBER THE LADIES."

1848: ELIZABETH CADY STANTON'S DECLARATION OF SENTIMENTS IS ADOPTED IN SENECA FALLS, NEW YORK.

1851: SOJOURNER TRUTH DELIVERS HER "AIN'T I A WOMAN?" SPEECH.

1920: THE NINETEENTH AMENDMENT GUARANTEES WOMEN THE RIGHT TO VOTE.

1948: THE UN ISSUES THE UNIVERSAL DECLARATION OF HUMAN RIGHTS.

1963: BETTY FRIEDAN PUBLISHES *THE FEMININE MYSTIQUE.*

1971: THE NATIONAL WOMEN'S POLITICAL CAUCUS IS FOUNDED. *OUR BODIES, OURSELVES* APPEARS WITH THIS NAME.

1979: THE UN ADOPTS THE CONVENTION ON THE ELIMINATION OF ALL FORMS OF DISCRIMINATION AGAINST WOMEN.

1993: THE UN DECLARES THAT "WOMEN'S RIGHTS ARE HUMAN RIGHTS."

2017: #METOO TAKES OFF ON SOCIAL MEDIA.

2018: THE TIME'S UP MOVEMENT BEGINS.

GLOSSARY

activist: one who uses or supports strong actions to help make changes in politics or society

advocate: to support or speak in favor of something

American Civil War: a war in the United States fought between the North and the South from 1861 to 1865

assert: to say something in a strong way

caucus: a group of people who work together for a shared goal

discrimination: unfairly treating people unequally because of their race or beliefs

edition: the form in which something is published

humanism: a devotion to human welfare

impetus: a force that causes something to be done

inalienable: impossible to take away or give up

neurotic: tending to worry in ways that aren't healthy or reasonable

sexism: unfair treatment of women simply because they are women

suffrage: the right of voting

usurpation: the act of taking something, such as power, in a forceful way, especially without the right to do so

FOR MORE INFORMATION

BOOKS

Braun, Eric. *The Women's Rights Movement*. Minneapolis, MN: Lerner Publications, 2018.

Gillibrand, Kirsten. *Bold & Brave: Ten Heroes Who Won Women the Right to Vote*. New York, NY: Alfred A. Knopf, 2018.

Hopkinson, Deborah. *What Is the Women's Rights Movement?* New York, NY: Penguin Workshop, 2018.

WEBSITES

Declaration of Human Rights by Eleanor Roosevelt
www.unmultimedia.org/avlibrary/asset/1093/1093412/
Eleanor Roosevelt helped write the UN's Universal Declaration of Human Rights. Listen to her read the document.

Women of the World, Unite!
interactive.unwomen.org/multimedia/timeline/womenunite/en/index.html#/
Scroll through time to discover people and events in the struggle for women's rights.

Women's Rights
www.ushistory.org/us/26c.asp
Read about the birth of the women's rights movement in the United States.

INDEX